Penny Sue
The
Pure Hearted

by Serena DeGarmo

illustrated by Arielle De Marco

Penny Sue The Pure Hearted
DeWard Publishing Company, Ltd.
P.O. Box 6259, Chillicothe, Ohio 45601
800.300.9778
www.deward.com

Penny Sue The Pure Hearted is a work of fiction. Names, characters, places, and incidents are either a product of the author's imagination or are used fictitiously. Any resemblance to actual persons, living or dead, events, or locales is entirely coincidental.

Printed in the United States of America.

ISBN: 978-1-936341-55-9

This book is dedicated to my mom.
Thank you for introducing your little girl to Penny Sue.

Noah, Eliana, Jada, Keila, Adalena and Azaiah.
Thank you for giving Penny Sue new life and lots of
brothers and sisters.

"God blesses those whose hearts are pure, for they will see God." – Jesus

A friend loves at all times... – Proverbs 17.17

Jesus answered:
Love the Lord your God with all your heart, soul, and mind.
This is the first and most important commandment.
The second most important commandment is like this one.
And it is, "Love others as much as you love yourself." – Matthew 22.37–39

This is Penny Sue.

Penny Sue lives with her parents and her big brother Pete, her little sister
Penelope, and her baby sister Polly. Penny Sue loves being part of
her family. They are fun and happy, but most of all they love her a lot.
They also teach her about loving God.

9

Every day, the family rides to school together and prays for the day. Mom always says, "God, show us the people who need to see Your love today. Bless us as we walk into this school. Please let Your light shine through us."

And every day, Mom picks them up and says the same thing.
"Tell me something special about your day." Today Pete hollered that he got
an "A" on his spelling test and went on about a heated four-square match during recess.
Penelope sang Mom a new song about acorns that she learned in preschool. Usually
Penny Sue was eager to chime in, but today she sat quietly in the back seat of their van.

As they drove down the road, Mom looked in the mirror. "Penny Sue?" Mom waved her hand to get Penny Sue's attention. "How'd things go for you today?"

Penny Sue didn't say a word.

"Is something on your mind, Sweetie?"

Penny Sue sighed. "Yeah, we got a new girl today."

"Oh, you did?" Mom said. "Tell me about her."

"Well, her name is Harper. She came over from Mrs. Brown's room. She just moved here." Penny Sue sighed. "I think she's bad."

Surprised by Penny Sue's judgment, Mom asked, "Really? Why would you say that?"

"Mrs. Lynch said that we should help her make good choices in our room."

"Oh, I see," Mom said. "What do you think about that?"

"Hmm." Penny Sue looked up at the ceiling and curled her lips as she was thinking. "I think I should pray for her!" she said excitedly.

"Great idea!" Mom smiled.

That night when Dad tucked Penny Sue in, he read her a verse out of the Bible. "Dear friends, since God loved us that much, we surely ought to love each other."

"What does that mean Daddy?" Penny Sue gave him her usual look of curiosity.

"Let's see." Dad rubbed his chin as he thought. "It means that God loves us so very much. The way that we show God that we love Him back is to give His love to others."

Penny Sue smiled and gave Dad a big, squeezy hug. Dad kissed her good night and closed her door.

Penny Sue snuggled under her covers and folded her hands. "God, please be with the new girl, Harper. Help her to make good choices and be good at school. Oh, and… uh…help me to do what Daddy said tonight. Help me to give Your love to her." Little did she know that God was already answering Penny Sue's request.

Penny Sue was crushed.

That night in her room Penny Sue said, "Mom, I tried to talk to Harper today, but she wasn't very nice. I don't think she wants to be my friend."

Mom nodded and put her arm around Penny Sue. "Maybe. Or maybe she's had a lot of people not be very nice to her. Maybe that's why she doesn't always make good choices. I think you should keep trying."

With a deep breath Penny Sue said, "Ok."

Mom touched her cheek and added, "And I think you should keep praying."

As the next few days went by, Penny Sue tried to talk to Harper several times. She tried to share her peanut butter crackers during snack. She tried to tell Harper her favorite joke about a chocolate cow. She even asked her to play on the swings with her at recess. But every time Harper said, "No thanks." Every time she turned her head, and walked away. Until one day…

Penny Sue sat beside Harper at the craft table. Harper finished cutting her leaves and glued them onto a brown tree trunk made of construction paper. As Penny Sue cut her red, orange and yellow leaves, she mustered the courage to talk to Harper one more time. Penny Sue took a deep breath and said, "So, Harper where do you live?"

Slowly Harper looked up from her work.

Harper looked unsure. "Ah... I live with my grandma."

"Do you like it?" Penny Sue asked.

Harper shrugged. "Sort of, I guess. I really miss my old house."

"Oh," Penny Sue said looking down at her finished tree. "I'm sorry."

"It's ok. My Grandma's nice and all."

"Do you have your own room?"

"Yeah." Harper softened. This was the first time she felt like talking to someone about her move. The girls continued chatting until the teacher called them to line up for recess.

Later that afternoon when Penny Sue saw her mom waiting in front of the school, she ran toward her. She could hardly contain all the things she wanted to say. She nearly knocked her mother over. "MOM! You'll never guess what happened today."

"Tell me all about it," Mom said. As they walked through the parking lot Penny Sue told her mother everything that happened with Harper.

With words flying off her tongue, Penny Sue said, "Well, Harper lives with her Grandma. They live really close to us, Mom. She said that she would like to come over and play at our house some time. She lives there because her mom died in the summer..."

"Wait, what?" Mom grabbed her shoulder, interrupting Penny Sue.

"Yeah, I guess her mom got really sick this summer. She died, so Harper moved in with her Grandma. She said she would come play with me sometime, Mom! Then we played chase on the playground. It was really fun."

As Mom took in all this news, she shook her head with surprise. Penny Sue stood beside the van as Pete got Penelope in her seat. With thoughts jumbled in her head, Mom put Polly in her car seat. Then she turned back to look at Penny Sue. Finally, Mom placed her hand on the top of Penny Sue's head. She looked down at Penny Sue with joy, realizing how God had been working the whole time.

Tears filled Mom's eyes. "Penny Sue, I'm so proud of you."
In her heart Mom prayed a special prayer of thanks to their Father for
answering their little girl's small prayer in a big way. Mom continued,
"But most of all, God is really proud of you today."

Satisfied, Penny Sue smiled, grabbed her backpack and climbed into the van.

Draw your own picture of a time you had a problem with a friend.
How did it make you feel?

Devotional

*I remember when I was in grade school.
I had my feelings hurt a lot by a girl named Jill.
There were many times I came home from school crying
because she said such mean things to me. She got other girls to
be mean to me too and I even lost my best friend because
of her. Sadly, I didn't handle it like Penny Sue did. You see,
instead of praying for Jill, I became mean to her
and others like she was to me.*

*God's Word — the Bible — has a lot to say about the
kind of friend we need to be. Jesus said that while loving God
is the most important thing we can do, the next best thing is to
love people (Matthew 22.39). He even said that when someone is
mean to us we should be nice back to them (Matthew 7.12).*

*I think what Jesus meant was just what Penny Sue had done.
Even though Harper didn't want to talk to Penny Sue or play
with her, Penny Sue kept being nice. That's hard to do,
but it makes God really happy because that's how we
show our pure heart. Will you start today and join
Penny Sue by being pure hearted?*

Dear God,
You are big. And you are good.
I want to be full of love like you.
Can you please make my heart pure?
Help me to be kind to others.
When someone hurts my feelings,
show me how to be nice.
When someone is mean to me,
help me to not be mean back.
That's how I want to show you I love you.
Amen

"God blesses those who are poor and realize their need for him,
for the Kingdom of Heaven is theirs.
God blesses those who mourn,
for they will be comforted.
God blesses those who are humble,
for they will inherit the whole earth.
God blesses those who hunger and thirst for justice,
for they will be satisfied.
God blesses those who are merciful,
for they will be shown mercy.
God blesses those whose hearts are pure,
for they will see God.
God blesses those who work for peace,
for they will be called the children of God.
God blesses those who are persecuted for doing right,
for the Kingdom of Heaven is theirs"
Matthew 5.3–10.

CPSIA information can be obtained at www.ICGtesting.com
Printed in the USA
LVOW010712280113

317489LV00002B/2/P

9 781936 341559